Emotional Mastery Blueprint

How to Control Your Emotions To Improve Your Social Skills And Master Your Thoughts And Emotions

FREE DOWNLOAD

Sign Up For My Email List And Get The Ultimate Inner Peace Affirmation Audio Series To Attain Nirvana and Greater Peace for FREE!

Click here to get started: www.mikemccallister.com/list

Author's Note

Companion Animal Psychology

Thank you again for downloading this book!

Writing and speaking about the importance of inner peace and mental wellbeing has been closest to my heart, ever since 2017, when I lost my father. So much so, if there could be a point in time to see a sudden change in me, that would be it. Living in different continents and trying to get home in time as fast as a plane could go did not help. Unfortunately, I did not make it in time. I could not say my final good-bye. And I could not have all the conversations I thought of coming back to later.

The death of my father triggered a series of events in my personal life which not only affected my personal and professional relationships but shook me to the core leading to anxiety and panic attacks. As a result, my corporate poster boy rank was soon taken away and I was left to be a nobody which took its toll further.

Getting back was not easy. It took months of counselling, meditation and mindfulness to make peace with myself and others. But it was worth it. Along this journey my outlook on life changed. I realized that material pleasures are important but inner peace and mental wellbeing is priceless. And so, I began writing this series to help others chase the right things in life.

Also By Mike McCallister

Click here for my body of work: www.mikemccallister.com/books

- Steps to Finding Inner Peace and Happiness - How to Find Peace and Happiness Within Yourself (Buddha on the Inside Book 1)

- How To Meditate: Learn How To Meditate Step By Step And Reap The Benefits Of Meditation Everyday + Tips On How To Meditate Better (Buddha on the Inside Book 2)

- How To Be Mindful Of Thoughts: Steps To Achieving Mindfulness And Living In The Moment (Buddha on the Inside Book 3)

Thank you, and good luck!

against the publisher for any reparation, damages, or monetary loss due to the information herein, either directly or indirectly.

Respective authors own all copyrights not held by the publisher.

The information herein is offered for informational purposes solely and is universal as so. The presentation of the information is without a contract or any type of guarantee assurance.

The trademarks that are used are without any consent, and the publication of the trademark is without permission or backing by the trademark owner. All trademarks and brands within this book are for clarifying purposes only and are owned by the owners themselves, not affiliated with this document.

Table of Contents

Introduction

We are all trying to live a happy, fulfilling and meaningful life in everything we do. But as you well know, this happiness, fulfilment and meaning can be quite fleeting. This is especially when we have to deal with all manner of things that could make us angry, sad, disappointed and more.

But despite the many things that trigger our emotions and make it easy for us to 'lose it', some people are still able to take charge of their emotions. Some people can hold their cool even when the chips are down and are faced with all manner of challenges.

How do they do it?

How are they able to master their emotions even when they have every reason or justification to snap at colleagues, employees, customers etc.?

Simple - they leverage the power of emotional intelligence.

When you have emotional intelligence, you have the power to direct your life and the responses you give to different emotional stimuli in the best way possible, something that can give you an edge in so many facets of your life.

Indeed, as Tara Meyer Robson aptly put it:

"When attention is brought to an emotion, power is brought to your life."

If this sounds like something exciting, this book is about to show you exactly how you too can have the same level of mastery over your emotions, as the people that you admire having high levels of emotional intelligence.

In the end, you should be able to deal with any amount of work, social, financial and health challenges without breaking down emotionally.

Let's begin.

Chapter 1: An Overview of Emotional Mastery

Renowned science journalist and author, Daniel Goleman once said,

'If your emotional abilities aren't in hand, if you don't have self-awareness, if you are not able to manage your distressing emotions, if you can't have empathy and have effective relationships, then no matter how smart you are, you are not going to get very far.'

The truth is, if you do not have your thoughts and emotions in control, you are likely to overthink everything. You are also likely to read too much into every little occurrence or experience. In the end, you allow your emotions to get out of control when it is not necessary. You will act like a pressure cooker blowing its whistle and venting out your frustration on every other person.

Sadly, with unstable/volatile emotions, you will have a hard time living a stable, happy, and successful life that is free from drama.

You need to be calm, act rationally, relate well with people, and feel emotionally fulfilled to live a good life.

This happens when you have good control of your emotions, which is where emotional mastery comes in.

Let's learn more about that.

What is Emotional Mastery?

Emotional mastery simply entails being able to access or identify your emotions and then controlling them intelligently for your benefit. You can think of it as being conscious of the thoughts and emotions going through your mind and then using that knowledge to direct or mold the emotions the way you like.

We all have many thoughts going through our minds every single moment. These thoughts stir up different emotions that then create a state of mind referred to as the emotional state. For instance, after having a heated argument with your partner, you are likely to have an 'angry' emotional state.

Different emotions bring about different emotional states.

On themselves, emotions have no problem, as they are natural body reactions to different situations or stimuli. What matters is how we respond when different emotional states set in.

Continuing with the earlier example of having a heated argument with your partner- if you yell at him/ her, you will only prolong the fight with the two of you continually spewing venom at each other.

However, if only one of you controls their emotions by stepping back to unplug from the emotional rollercoaster, the fiery situation would quickly be extinguished. This is what emotional mastery is about, i.e., being completely aware of the different emotions you experience and acknowledging them to comprehend them better.

Instead of labeling an emotion as bad or negative, you choose to acknowledge it, accept it, and use it to your advantage.

But this does mean not in any way suggest you do not feel any emotion. It merely means accepting your emotions and understanding them better before moving forward with a particular action/response based on the feeling (s). For instance, when you are angry, you don't just get carried by the anger. You step back to notice your anger rising and then stop yourself from reacting angrily at the person or thing that made you angry. When you do that, you will see you no longer snap at people only to start apologizing shortly after when the damage is done.

What's more, you can channel the energy for whatever emotion you are taming towards something constructive.

Have you had countless instances where you have snapped on people or done anything you are embarrassed about as a result of responding emotionally?

If yes, you might wonder...

How can you take charge of your emotions if you have tried managing them with little or no success?

That's exactly what we are about to learn.

We will learn how to develop emotional mastery next, but before that, let me remind you why you should endeavor to establish this emotional mastery.

Chapter 2: Why it is Necessary to Control Our Emotions

Many experts in the fields of business, psychology, and interpersonal relationships agree that EQ (emotional quotient), also referred to as emotional intelligence (EI) is a more critical measure of your success in life as compared to Intelligence Quotient (IQ).

Yes, your IQ might have gotten you good SAT scores, which may have subsequently landed you your dream job. However, working on that dream job is going to require much more than your IQ. You have to know how to deal with pressure from people, the job, your family, health, and more. If you don't know how to manage your emotions well as you deal with people, you are likely to be overwhelmed and frustrated.

A high EI helps you maintain healthy relationships, be able to get better career opportunities at work, achieve your personal and professional goals, and be the true boss of your life. Just think about it; everyone would want to recommend someone warm, emotionally intelligent, etc. when an opportunity comes up. Not someone snappy.

If you don't have good relations with the people you work with or for, you can bet that you will be stuck at the same position for far too long. Progressing in your career (especially into leadership positions) requires that you be able to handle pressure from everywhere and still maintain your cool. Nobody will want you to lead if they know you have a problem managing pressure and people.

Let me walk you through all the different reasons why it is essential to master your thoughts and emotions.

Helps You Make Well-Informed Decisions

EI can make the difference between making hasty emotionally driven decisions and making informed decisions after analyzing all possible scenarios.

I'll give you an example to explain this:

Imagine a situation where there is an open job position within your company that may pay more, allow you to travel the world for work, and more.

At first, if you are reacting emotionally, you may just jump to the opportunity without thinking through what the opportunity entails. You may not think about how the job may mean you won't get to spend as much time with your children, spouse, and friends. It may mean you have to miss out on your kids' critical years. It may mean you may grow apart from your spouse. It may mean longer working hours and more.

The above is just an example to illustrate how making hasty decisions based on emotions can turn out.

Another example may be a situation where your boss assigns a new, reasonably challenging project to you. If you let your thoughts and emotions take over, you may end up not getting the project done to your boss' satisfaction. You may feel he/she only assigns the complicated projects to you to frustrate you or to make you fail. You may also think your boss likes overburdening you with work when there are equally capable people. But if you put your emotions aside, you may realize that your boss wants you to grow and master a particular skill. They may also be grooming you for more responsibilities.

Having emotional mastery allows you to step back and consider a situation before acting on them. This, in turn, ensures you make informed, well thought out decisions.

Helps You Build Meaningful, Healthy Relationships

Having emotional mastery can improve your relationships significantly. With EI, you won't snap at colleagues (juniors or superiors) at work or hold grudges against your boss but will keep your peace while dealing with angry customers, and much more. With EI, you will be able to spot when your boss, colleague, or even customer is going through something in life and be able to offer the much-needed support during that phase. You will be able to tell when they are celebrating special moments and celebrate with them as well.

All that will help you build and nurture relationships at your place of work and outside work and will, without a doubt, go a long way in your career prospects.

Manage and Lead Team Members

Emotional mastery is a must-have if you wish to become more successful in your profession.

Whether you are employed or you run a business, you will be interacting with people. As such, you need to build a good rapport with your boss, colleagues, team members, subordinates, customers, suppliers, etc..

The only way you can grow, get better opportunities, and have successful collaborations is by touching people's lives through your emotional mastery. You celebrate successes/highs with all relevant people and don't let any lows that may come mess up the otherwise good relationship you have built, which is the best way to build strong relationships with members of your team to work towards a common goal.

When you have EI, you will not snap at your juniors for making mistakes, not take criticism personally or hold grudges. You will relate well with customers and suppliers, no matter the situation without losing your cool.

With proper emotional mastery, you will know how to manage your anger and act sensibly irrespective of the circumstances. Instead of fuming at team members or getting into a row with colleagues, you will come off as the bigger, wiser person during arguments to get your message across effectively and calmly.

It will be easier to influence people towards a specific goal or course when they know they can trust you, and when they see that you don't let emotions get in the way of work. Nobody will think you have anything against them when you relate with them well and are there for them during the highs and lows.

Helps You Understand Your Aspirations Better

If you feel as if your life lacks meaning, perhaps what you may be having is a lack of emotional intelligence than anything else.

Let me explain:

When you struggle with EI, you let superficial emotions (which tend to be very fleeting) take over the center stage of your life. You dwell on them as they are and magnify them to make them much bigger.

But when you have mastery of your emotions, you don't just dwell on them. You dig deep to understand where they have stemmed from and what is the root cause.

Let's use our example of feeling that your life and work lacks meaning and is boring. Digging deeper into your life will reveal the real reason why you feel the way you feel.

Ask yourself; do you feel your life or work is boring because:

- You do the same thing over and over again in your place of work?

- You no longer find your job as stimulating?

- You spend too much time at your place of work?

- Is it that you don't let yourself to have fun after work and all you think about is work even when you are at home?

- You don't have a good relationship with your colleagues, and you feel bored just not having anyone to talk during office meetings or happy hours?

- You've not been able to engage in your hobbies or advance in your studies because of work?

These are some excellent questions that you can use to dig deeper into the reason for the kind of emotions you are experiencing to know the root course. After finding answers to these questions (it is good to note them down in a book or journal), you can choose to address the real issue that is making you have the emotions.

Having a mastery of your emotions makes you more than just a whiner and a thinker but someone that acts on whatever deep-seated issues are going through your mind.

The more you try to understand yourself and your thoughts, the better you become aware of what you truly yearn for. This enables you to set meaningful goals, find your life's purpose, and steer your life in the right direction. Such is the beauty of understanding your thoughts and emotions.

For all these reasons and the fact that taming your emotions helps you embrace the present and all the blessings it entails, it is crucial to master your thoughts and emotions.

Let us now move further along to learn about different strategies to build your EI.

Is this book helping you in some way? If so, I'd love to hear about it. Your honest reviews would help readers find the right book for their needs and help me tailor the future books to yours. Reviews are the single most important factor in determining if a book succeeds, so I'm incredibly thankful for people like you who I can rely on to leave one.

Click here to leave a review for this book on your favorite online store: www.mikemccallister.com/books or click here to leave a review on Goodreads: www.mikemccallister.com/goodreads

Chapter 3: The Emotional Triad

To have complete emotional mastery, you should know that your emotions and feelings are dependent on three essential factors, which are referred to as the 'Emotional Triad.'

Your Physiology

Any and every emotion that you experience is felt inside your body first, which means if you want to induce a particular emotion, you should take on the physiology of that specific emotion.

If you wish to feel confident, stand tall with your chest and shoulders open and broad. Speak clearly and loudly, and you will start feeling confident. Similarly, if you frown, breathe shallow and murmur, you will soon feel sad.

Your physiology largely determines the emotions you feel. Hence, you need to improve on it to experience the desired emotions and control intense emotions.

Always remember that emotion is produced by motion, so if you take the right motion, you build the right emotion.

Things You Focus On

Henry Ford aptly put it, *"Whether you think you can, or you think you can't – you're right."*

Whatever you focus on becomes your reality. Fixating on the negatives associated with a situation disturbs you from within. If your boss insulted you for shoddy work and you don't let go of that memory, you will ruminate on the agony those words triggered and feel miserable from within.

Not only will you experience a strong emotion of sadness, but when you fixate on a specific thought and feeling for long, you feed it in your subconscious mind.

Your subconscious embraces that suggestion and creates more similar thoughts. Your thoughts can travel in the universe and draw other thoughts and even experiences with a similar vibrational frequency towards them. Sad, upsetting, and anger filled thoughts have a low vibrational frequency and so draw same thoughts and experiences your way. This is why when you are upset, angry, frustrated, or scared, you only attract more of such experiences your way, and then that becomes your reality.

On the contrary, if you choose to focus on the positives associated with an experience, you will feel better about yourself and your life. You will instantly shift your state of mind to a positive from a negative one, and focus on things that help you feel better.

Naturally, this enables you to nurture positive beliefs and then channelize their power to draw better experiences your way.

To master your thoughts and emotions, you should shift your attention from the upsetting, frustrating, and unhealthy aspects to the healthier and more constructive ones. If you are feeling angry, think of what your anger is trying to teach you instead of what you have lost because of your anger. Similarly, if you wish to be happy, ask yourself what you need to be happy and start working towards improving that aspect.

Your Language

Your language comprises of the words and tone you use while speaking to yourself and others. It, along with your physiology and focus, plays a massive role in shaping, exacerbating, calming, and controlling your emotions.

The words you speak, particularly those that you use frequently, become embedded in your mind. Naturally, when you continuously give specific suggestions to yourself, you focus on precisely that. When you focus on something, you draw similar experiences your way and materialize that particular reality.

Every word has a different emotional state attached to it. The word 'tired' is likely to make you feel exhausted and withdrawn; the word 'difficult' is likely to upset and demotivate you, and the word 'hate' is likely to trigger anger.

Different words make up different phrases and sentences, and the way you use them affects your mood and emotions in that very moment. If you keep telling yourself how you will never be happy, you will only feel dejected and withdrawn.

Mastering your emotions requires you to master your language and have a language that is empowering. This regularly lifts your spirits and improves your emotional state. Instead of using disempowering phrases and speech, incorporate the right words in your everyday language. This way, you continuously feed healthy and constructive statements, words, phrases, and metaphors in your mind. For that to happen, first be aware of the language you use and improve on it consciously.

Every emotional mastery technique uses this emotional triad to help you first accept, understand, embrace, acknowledge, and then improve on your emotions. In your routine life too, pay attention to the triad and use these elements to calm down an aggravated emotional state and then turn it into a more empowering one.

The first step to master your thoughts and emotions is to become mindful of yourself and your surroundings. The next chapter discusses this technique in detail and will teach you strategies to nurture mindfulness.

Chapter 4: Cultivate Complete Mindfulness

"The present is the only reality and the only certainty."

— Arthur Schopenhauer

If you wish to truly break the cycle of letting emotions take over your thoughts and actions, you have to stay in the present. And the best way to stay in your present is to practice mindfulness.

Mindfulness refers to the ability to live in the moment and accept everything it entails peacefully, nonjudgmentally, and acceptingly. It is an essential ingredient if you want to become emotionally intelligent and improve your wellbeing as well.

How is being present and practicing mindfulness related to becoming emotionally intelligent, you may wonder?

Let me explain that.

Mindfulness allows you to embrace every moment as you experience it, along with everything it brings forth. Instead of worrying about what could have been or what was, you focus on what is in the moment and accept it nonjudgmentally.

For example, if you find out you did not get the promotion you were hoping for, you don't let the emotion of disappointment or anger take over your life and affect your work after that. Instead, you focus primarily on what you can do at that moment to be happy instead of complaining about the situation.

Similarly, if you feel angry, you do not fixate on the problem and ruminate on it, as that will only make you more furious. Instead, you accept the anger as your emotion. However, you choose not to respond angrily. You decide to let the anger take its course until you calm down - without reacting angrily.

As a result, you become more mindful of yourself and your surrounding environment. Moreover, you understand yourself, your thoughts, your emotions, and your aspirations better as well as how the surrounding environment influences you.

You learn to be accepting of yourself and your emotions and treat them as fleeting feelings that are likely to fade away if you allow them to. This keeps you from holding tight onto emotions and wreaking unnecessary havoc in your mind and life. Naturally, this is an ongoing process- one that requires time and patience. However, if you keep at it and adopt the right strategies, you can become more mindful and emotionally intelligent with time.

Here are some powerful ways to cultivate a mindful state of mind.

Meditate Regularly

Meditation is arguably the most exceptional tool to cultivate mindfulness as it helps you anchor to the present, by bringing your awareness onto your breath, thoughts, emotion, sound, suggestion, or word.

When you meditate, you slowly divert your attention from the past or future concerns to the present moment. This trains you to focus on the here and now, and become more aware of your thoughts and emotions. As you focus on them better, you understand them better in an unbiased manner. And as your focus and physiology improve, your emotional state improves as well.

While there are many meditative techniques, here is a super simple one for novices to begin with. It is known as *mindfulness-based breathing meditation.*

- Sit somewhere quiet and settle down.

- Close your eyes if you want to and place your hands on your sides.

- Breathe in your natural manner, but inhale through your nose and exhale via your mouth.

- Very gently, bring your awareness onto your breath and calmly watch your breath as you inhale and exhale it. Pay close attention to how the air circulates in your body, produces different movements and sensations, and then exits your system.

- Keep watching your breath for two full minutes.

- Every time you wander off in thought, acknowledge that thinking has occurred and bring back your attention to your breath. Be patient with yourself, and do not judge yourself every time you drift off into thought. This slowly teaches you to be nonjudgmental towards everything, including your emotions and practice acceptance all the time.

- When the two minutes are over, gently open your eyes and resume your daily chores with mindfulness.

Practice this exercise daily for 2 minutes, and you'll be amazed at how calm you feel. You then need to extend this awareness to your emotions and everything around you to become more accepting of everything.

This practice teaches you to shift your focus from whatever upsets you to your breath to relax. The techniques that follow below will require this fundamental awareness, which is why we have learned how to meditate first.

Be Mindful of Your Emotions

The reason why we allow certain emotions to exacerbate is that we aren't often mindful of their existence. This makes us unconsciously hold onto them and allow them to create chaos inside us. Moreover, we have a habit of reacting to everything instead of calmly observing the situation and responding later.

Now that you wish to attain complete emotional mastery, it is time to change things for the better.

- Pay attention to the different symptoms of different emotions you experience in various situations. For instance, you may get a headache when you feel angry, or your shoulders may start to feel heavy when you feel stressed out. Observe these symptoms so that you can spot the onset of intense emotions before they become a problem.

- Once you identify a particular emotion stirring inside you, excuse yourself from the situation. Sit somewhere peaceful, and observe the feeling calmly.

- Practice mindfulness breathing meditation taught above to divert your attention from the tons of thoughts that may be upsetting you. Become grounded in the moment.

- Once you feel more aware of the moment and the emotions you are experiencing, observe it gently and sit tight.

- Let the emotion stir inside you, rise to a certain point, and then subside on its own. If you just stay with it and do not react to it, it won't cause any harm at all.

- You may experience reactive thoughts such as yelling at someone or punching the wall or behaving violently with someone who has hurt you. However, you need to gently shrug off these thoughts and just stay with your emotion.

- The most intense emotion lasts for only 12 minutes if you do not hold onto it. This means if you feel angry or scared for weeks and months, it is actually us who aren't letting it go away. If you stay calm and do not react to the emotion, it will fade away on its own in 12 minutes, leaving you settled and free. Give yourself and that emotion those 12 minutes, and you will be surprised at how light you feel.

Practice this technique every time you find a strong emotion setting in and you'll gently relax it within minutes. You train yourself to improve your sense of focus and physiology by staying calm and peaceful, which consequently stabilizes your emotional state.

Respond and Not React

Once your emotion has calmed down, you need to then mindfully think of the most appropriate way to take the next step forward. This is known as 'responding to the emotion' and is an extremely rational way of managing your emotions.

Here is an example:

Let's assume one of the employees did something irresponsible that made you lose business. If you fixate on your anger, you may react irrationally and later regret your behavior.

At this point, allow your anger to subside and then think of the best way to go forward instead of firing them immediately. You can practice deep breathing meditation to calm down and not react angrily.

If you feel letting go of them is the best approach to pursue after thoroughly assessing the situation, so be it. However, if there is another approach you can take, try that first.

Similarly, you may want to call off your business partnership with a specific partner after getting into a quarrel with him/her. However, if you let your boiling rage cool off, you are likely to realize the two of you need to discuss the matter keeping your emotions aside to reach a mutual agreement.

Give yourself those 10 to 15 minutes with a specific intense emotion, be it that of happiness, anger, or sadness to observe and understand it so that you respond to it and not react. Once you start responding to your emotions, you make well-informed decisions and then better manage those around you as well. This works particularly well in workplace situations.

Mindfully Accept and Improve on Your Thoughts

Your thoughts often breed certain emotions, and your language largely influences your thoughts. To master your emotions, you need to train yourself to pay attention to your thoughts and then replace the toxic ones with healthier ones by improving your language.

- If you feel a specific intense emotion upsets you, trace back the thought that may have induced that emotion. If you feel stressed, what is it that you thought of a few minutes ago? Maybe you said something demeaning to yourself, or perhaps you are still thinking of the hurtful things your father said to you? Dig deep to know the connection between your thoughts and emotions.

- Next, accept the fact that something hurtful was said, but it does not exist at the moment anymore.

- If it is something you said to yourself, you need to improve on your self-talk. If you thought, 'I can never be happy,' change it to, 'I am happy with myself and my life.' If you thought, 'I always fail,' change it to, 'I am doing well and will achieve my targets.' Replace every negative thought with something positive and chant it over and over again. Within minutes, you will feel better and soon develop the habit of talking to yourself at all times positively.

- If someone else said something disturbing to you, accept the fact that you cannot change people, but can only control your sense of focus and perception. Accept it as a bygone while focusing on what the experience has taught you. If someone told you that you don't work hard, analyze the statement objectively. If you don't work hard, accept your weakness and improve on it. In this manner, you train yourself to pick out the positives from every situation and focus on becoming better.

- Moreover, use words with a positive connotation with everyone. This ensures you talk courteously and respectfully with others and yourself. This positively influences people around you, keeps them calm, and helps you come off as the more poised, positive, emotionally stronger person.

If you consistently work on these strategies, you will start feeling emotionally calm at all times. The next chapter shares

with you some more exciting approaches to further control
your thoughts and emotions.

Chapter 5: Fun Games and Techniques to Improve Emotional Intelligence

Learning something becomes super-exciting when you incorporate fun games and techniques in the equation. Here are some interesting and enjoyable games and methods to develop and nurture emotional intelligence mastery.

The Superman/Wonder Woman Technique

Research shows that your body language influences your confidence and happiness levels. This also reinforces the fact that your physiology affects your emotional state.

Poses wherein you stand tall, broaden your shoulders, and maintain eye contact with others are known as high power body poses. They improve the testosterone levels in your body that boosts your confidence and enthusiasm.

On the other hand, if you practice low power body poses wherein you slouch, do not maintain eye contact, close your limbs, and lower your head, you lower your testosterone levels. This reduces your confidence and enthusiasm, making you feel sad and demotivated.

An interesting game to build the habit of having a high power body language to develop a positive emotional state is to act like superman/wonder woman.

- Stand tall and straight and open your hips and shoulders.

- Keep your feet shoulder-width apart.

- Raise your chin and head and look straight confidently.

- Place your arms at your waist and stand proud.

- Maintain this pose for 2 minutes, and you will start to feel a buzz of confidence inside you.

Practice this pose twice a day, and whenever you feel low, and you'll instantly brighten up.

Play the 'I Did It' Game

This game is best played in a group of 3 to 5 people, but you can also do it on your own or with a good friend. It helps you recall positive scenarios in your life when you accomplished an obstacle by staying calm and allows you to induce that emotional state to take better charge of your life.

- If you are playing it in a group, ask someone to play hooks of musical themes from popular movies such as Mission Impossible, Batman, Superman, etc.

- Every participant needs to take 5 minutes to recall a time in their life when they encountered an obstacle. Also, think of how you overcame it with resilience, perseverance, and positivity.

- Imagine yourself emerging as the superhero in the situation and saving the day.

- Think of the obstacle, the goal, and how you stood up to the occasion and proved your mettle.

- If you are playing this game alone, you need to play the musical hook yourself and recall that experience wherein you did not allow your emotions to get the better of you.

- Play the game 3 to 5 times in a go, and you will feel a lot more focused and emotionally stronger than before.

You can even write down that account in your journal and go through it frequently to remind yourself of your emotional strength to slowly train yourself to act powerfully in tensile situations.

Emotional Bubble Bursting Game

This super fun and easy game will help you relax when you find your emotions getting out of control.

- Sit peacefully and give the specific emotion you wish to soothe a particular color. If you feel angry, you could give it a red or orange color.

- Imagine that emotion wrapped in a red-colored bubble and growing bigger as you experience it strongly.

- When it becomes incredibly large, take a deep breath and imagine bursting that bubble with a prickly needle.

- As you exhale, imagine all the anger leaving your body.

- Practice it 5 to 10 times, and you'll feel serene within minutes.

Try this game with different emotions to promote a peaceful state of mind quickly.

Apps to Build Emotional Intelligence

Here are some cool apps that you can download to improve your emotional intelligence and also help your kids build it.

- <u>Calm</u>: This is a super cool and relaxing app that helps you build a peaceful state of mind and keep your intense emotions under control.

- <u>Breathe, Think, Do With Sesame</u>: While this game is mainly designed for kids, it works well for adults too. It takes you on a trip down the memory lane, reminds you of your favorite show as a kid, and teaches you to calm your emotions simultaneously.

- <u>Mindful Powers</u>: This game requires you to take care of an adorable creature to attain self-control and build more positive emotional states.

- <u>Stop, Breathe & Think</u>: This is a lovely app that promotes compassion and acceptance. You take timeouts to reflect on your thoughts frequently, which helps you identify rational ways to act in stressful situations.

Conclusion

You are amazing; it is about time you realized that. Harness that power and use it to build a peaceful life.

This book has equipped you with every strategy you need to achieve this goal. Now take action!

We shall continue to dive deeper in the next volume of this series. There, we'll explore uncharted territories, unravel hidden truths, and ignite your potential even further.

Thank you for being part of this journey. Your amazing future awaits.

Did this book help you in some way? If so, I'd love to hear about it. Your honest reviews would help readers find the right book for their needs and help me tailor the future books to yours. Reviews are the single most important factor in determining if a book succeeds, so I'm incredibly thankful for people like you who I can rely on to leave one.

Click here to leave a review for this book on your favorite online store: www.mikemccallister.com/books or click here to leave a review on Goodreads: _www.mikemccallister.com/goodreads_

FREE DOWNLOAD

Sign Up For My Email List And Get The Ultimate Inner Peace Affirmation Audio Series To Attain Nirvana and Greater Peace for FREE!

Click here to get started: www.mikemccallister.com/list